Walter Wangerin, Jr.

Angels &
All Children

A Nativity Story in Words, Music, and Art

Illustrated by Tim Ladwig ✦ Music by Randy Courts

To my grandchildren
with shining eyes
I dedicate this story,
Emma Michele and Maxwell David

Once, long ago—ten years, times one hundred years, plus one thousand years: *that* long ago—people were walking in darkness. People were living in a land so dark that the day was the same as the night.

They couldn't tell the difference because they had turned away from God—and God *is* light! The people stopped loving God. Instead, they loved themselves the more and the more and the most. Each person covered his sight and said, "Who's more important than I am? No one can tell *me* what to do. Don't need rules. Don't need commandments. And I most certainly don't need God!"

But this is the same as saying, "I don't need the sun in the sky."

So the people covered their land with a darkness darker than night, a dark *so* dark and a night *so* long that a terrible sadness followed: the children went to bed.

All the children went to sleep.

And none of the children woke up again. They *couldn't* wake up, because the morning wasn't coming back. Until the sun rose up in the sky, the children would sleep and sleep and sleep. . . .

So then it was that the adults who had caused the darkness became lonely. Lonely and sad, because they missed the children. They cried: "We miss your laughter, your happy chatter, your hugs and your love and your trust. When, oh, when," the parents said, "will you come back to us?"

But even though they didn't love him, God was in love with the people.

God looked down from heaven and saw that the earth was stuck like a clock at midnight. "No, no, this is not good," he said. "It's time to make time tick again, time to turn the land from night to morning."

God saw how lonely the people were for their children. He felt their sorrow in the darkness they had caused; so he said, "It's time to do a new thing, and to do it now!"

God so loved the world that he sent his only Son into the world itself. And this is how he did it:

"Gabriel?" he called to his bright archangel. "Gabriel?"

And the angel said, "Here, Lord. Here I am. What do you want me to do?"

> *"Gabriel, down—go down*
> *With my favor*
> *Now and ever;*
> *Fly to my Mary: say*
> *She'll deliver a child, a son.*
>
> *"'Jesus' his name must be,*
> *Great as David,*
> *Savior ever;*
> *Tell her my Spirit will move*
> *Like the morning within her womb."*

Suddenly there was an angel flying through the night, swiftly, silently, over the oceans, down to a province named Galilee, down to a city named Nazareth, down to a house in that city, down to a woman in that house—

down,
        down to Mary,
                young and blameless,
                sleeping in bed.

The angel came like light.

The angel grew very, very bright and said:

"HAIL, MARY, YOU FAVORITE OF GOD! THE LORD IS WITH YOU!"

Mary awoke, shaking with terror.

"Thunder? Lightning?" she cried. She sat up, her hand on her mouth. "Is it storming?" she whispered. "What is coming to me?"

When God saw how scared she was, he leaned down and whispered, "Hurry, Gabriel! Comfort young Mary. Give her the good news *quietly*."

So the angel said to Mary, "Hush, hush, don't be afraid. God loves you, Mary. You are going to conceive and bear a son and name him 'Jesus.' He will be great; he will be the son of the Highest, and he will sit on the throne of David and reign over the house of Jacob forever."

"Excuse me? Angel?" Mary said. "I'm sorry, but it can't happen."

"What can't happen?"

"Well, maybe angels don't know how people have babies," she said. "I myself, I can't have one, on account of, I'm not married. I don't have a husband."

The angel chuckled. The angel took a cosmic breath and laughed a thundersome laugh—because the thing that he was telling her, well, it was a miracle after all.

"The Holy Spirit will come upon you, Mary," he said. "The power of the Most High will overshadow you, so the child to be born of you will be holy. He will be called the Son of God. Mary? Mary, with God nothing is impossible."

Mary couldn't speak a while. Her eyes were sparkling with the light of joy. A baby? A baby!

Finally she whispered, "Oh, yes. Yes! With all my heart I want to serve the Lord, so let it be to me according to your word."

A baby! Mary was going to have *God's* baby. . . .

When the angel had gone from her, Mary rose up on her toes. She spread her arms wide, and then she turned her joy into words, and she turned the words into beautiful singing.

And Mary said, "He remembered me.
He remembered his maiden of low degree:
With tender care and gentility
  He remembered me.

"I breathe, and my breathing laughs in the Lord;
I live, and my life enlarges his name;
For I have heard his mighty word,
Obeyed his bright, genetic word,
And I that Word contain. . . ."

And Mary said, "He remembers me.
From my silence and my singularity
He lifts his maid from her low degree;
  He remembers me.

"But all of the women, all of the men,
All of the children, fearing his name—
He mercies them, God mercies them,
Reveals his strong right arm to them,
And sweeps the rich away. . . ."

And Mary said, "He remembers you!
He will lead you, exalt you, and love you, too.
Children of old, O be children new!
  He remembers you.

"And who are the full? God gives them no food.
And where are the hungry? He fills them with good.
The powerful by God shall fall
The proud remember how to crawl,
The poor rise up renewed. . . ."

And Mary said, "He remembers well
All the promises made unto Isra'el.
To Abraham and to us he swore
*   Love forevermore."*

And Mary said, "He remembers me;
He has made me the place of the Savior-seed.
Oh, let it be, Lord, that I, like you,
Will remember, too.
I will remember you . . . too."

In that long, long night when the children were sleeping, the adults couldn't see each other very well. Faces were shadows, and hearts were in shadow, too. In darkness, then, neither could they understand each other. Even if they were in love, there was such a darkness between them that one couldn't know what the other one was thinking.

This is what happened to Joseph, the man who was engaged to marry Mary.

He loved her. And he was sure that she loved him. And they planned to live together. Yes, yes, but Joseph started to see some changes in Mary which he could not understand.

"Mary," he said, "why are you smiling all the time?"

"Oh, you'll see," she said. "Soon you will see."

"But why are you giggling? Why do you laugh? Why do you make so many jokes with me? And what is that strange light in your eyes?"

"Oh, you'll see. Soon you will see."

"Stop it!" Joseph commanded her. "Don't giggle! Don't laugh. Because I know what's going on, and it is not funny!" Joseph was frowning now, a dark, dark, midnight frown. "You're going to have a baby, aren't you, Mary? And I am not the father! Oh, Mary! Mary, what have you done? How could you do this to me?"

"But Joseph," she said, "it wasn't me. It was the Holy Spirit."

"Woman, you're making it worse and worse!" he scolded. "Now you're lying to me, and you are blaspheming God. Please, please, have the decency to tell me the truth."

But miserable Mary could only say, "It was the Holy Spirit."

So Joseph turned away from her. He walked the road to his own home, thinking: "She's lying. No, Mary doesn't love me anymore. She loves somebody else instead."

In those days the dark world had some dark and hurtful rules. According to those rules, a man could put a woman away from him—and then it would be as if they had never talked of marriage at all. This was the law. If a woman had a baby by somebody besides the man she was to marry, he could put her away.

And that's what Joseph decided to do.

As he climbed in bed, he said, "I hate this. Oh, but I have to do it. Tomorrow I will put Mary away from me forever. Quietly. Privately. I will not shame her the way she's shaming me. I will not tell everyone in town. . . ."

And so he fell into a lonesome and sorrowful sleep.

But God knew what Joseph was feeling. God always knew when friends and lovers were torn apart, and he felt the pain of their broken hearts.

So he called to his angel. "Gabriel?" he said.

And Gabriel answered, "Here, Lord. Here I am. What do you want me to do?"

"Gabriel, go down. Go down in the darkness to a man in a small town. . . .

"Joseph is sleeping now,
   Sadly, lonely,
   Lost his Mary:
Joseph believes she loves
Someone better than she loves him.

"Go to him, Gabriel,
   In his sleeping,
   Be his dreaming:
Tell him that Mary's child
Is from Heaven, Emmanuel!

"Tell him to marry her
   Just as soon as
   He awakens,
Blessing, protecting her,
For the baby is God's! God's Son!"

Suddenly there was an angel flying through the night, over the oceans, down to Galilee, down to the city of Nazareth, to a second house in that

"Joseph," the angel said. "Joseph, son of David."

The light came into Joseph's sleeping, growing brighter and brighter, the brightness of a very good dream.

"Joseph," said Gabriel, "don't be afraid to bring Mary home as your wife. For the child in her is from the Holy Spirit, exactly as she told you. She'll bear a son whom you must name 'Jesus'—because he will save his people from their sins."

He will save: he will save his people from their sins. Well, of course! The darkness had come from sinning in the first place. So, if the baby named Jesus can take away the sins of the people, he will take away the darkness, too. This is the most beautiful truth of all: that the baby born to Mary was going to be the light of the whole wide world!

Joseph woke up with a broad grin on his face! He rushed out into the streets grinning so broadly that his whole face seemed to glow. And he giggled!

When the people heard him, and when they saw the sunburst smile in his face, they were bothered. "Joseph," they said, "you were always a sober, a diligent man, and we looked up to you. But this is different. This is silly—and you are changing."

"Yes! Yes," cried Joseph. "Isn't it wonderful?"

But they said, "Why are you smiling?"

And he answered, "Oh, you'll see. Soon you will see."

"Joseph," they scolded him, "you're a grown man! Why would a grown man giggle? Why do you laugh? And what is that strange light coming from your face?"

"Oh, you'll see," he said. "Soon you will see."

"Well, stop it!" they cried. "Don't laugh! Life is serious, not funny."

But Joseph was already running swiftly to Mary's house, calling, "Yes it is! Life is wonderful, because love is coming again!"

When he got to Mary's house, he beat on the door. He heard tiny feet creeping inside, then the door was opened just a crack, and Joseph saw Mary's eye peeping out. There was a tear there, but whether for sadness or for gladness, Joseph didn't know. So he started to speak. He started to sing:

> *"Mary, I'll build you a little home*
> *Where three of us can dwell.*
> *The roof will be straw and the walls will be stone*
> *To keep you very well.*
>
> *"I'll make you a cradle for your child*
> *To rock him to and fro;*
> *And if he should waken and cry a while,*
> *I'll stroke him top to toe.*
>
> *"Board for a table, canes for a chair,*
> *Copper for pots and plates;*
> *I'll furnish your kitchen with dinnerware*
> *And bake you barley cakes. . . ."*

Now Mary's door was opened wide, and she was standing there with her two hands over her mouth, and the tears were just pouring down her fingers.

So Joseph grabbed one wet hand and kneeled down before the young woman, singing, singing:

"Oh, Mary! Mary, marry me,
    And I'll provide you both
With everything your bodies need . . .
    Till God requires a death.

"I'll be to Jesus fatherly,
    Until that Father calls
Whose roof is all eternity,
    And mountains are his walls.

"And then I'll build one other thing,
    A box to fit a grave,
A place to lay your Baby-King
    Who came the world to save."

Mary slipped to her own knees now and put her arms around Joseph. She lay her cheek beside his cheek, so that his singing was softer and softer and only Mary could hear him sing:

> *"I'll hold you, Mary, heaven's queen,*
> *Until your child awakes,*
> *Raised by the Builder of everything*
> *In three primeval days."*

Suddenly Joseph stood up and raised Mary up, too, and threw back his head and sang the next verse with a very loud love:

> *"Then fly! Then fly! Oh, Mary, fly*
> *From here to paradise;*
> *Your son's the Son of the Most High:*
> *Oh, go to him, the Christ. . . ."*

Joseph put his left arm around Mary's shoulders and began to lead her up the road to his own small house, there to be his wife.
    And as they went, he sang:

> *"Mary, I've hammered a little home*
> *Where three of us can live.*
> *My roof is but straw, and my walls are mere stone*
> *The best that I can give*
> *Until you have to leave. . . ."*

ow it came to pass in those dark days and lonesome days, that Caesar Augustus, the king of the world, turned to his soldiers and said, "It's time. Time to make a list of all the people in my kingdoms. Go forth," he said to his generals, his sergeants, and soldiers. "Go forth and command the people to return to the cities of their ancestors, and when they have gathered, count them! Ten, one hundred, one thousand, count them all!"

So everyone went to be counted, everyone to his own city.

Joseph also went up from Galilee, out of the province of Nazareth, into the province of Judea, unto the city of David named "Bethlehem," because he was a great-great-great grandson of King David. He went to be counted with Mary, his young bride, who was big with her baby. She was almost ready to deliver.

As they went up the stony roads, they sang soft questions together:

"Bethlehem, Bethlehem,
 God is coming!
 Are you ready?
Innkeeper, have you room
For a mother to bear her son?"

Ah, but the city lay in darkness. Joseph knocked on many doors. But every innkeeper only said, "No," and "No," and "No, we have no room for you."

Down into a little cave he led his Mary. Down to where the animals fed on hay. And there he laid her safely down.

Ah, Mary: she groaned deep and deep within her body, rocking to help the baby come out.

Then all at once the tiny Jesus slipped into the world, and the light of the Son burst into the cave, as if God had said, *Let there be light!*

And Mary wrapped her baby in swaddling clothes and laid him on hay in a manger.

God the Father was laughing now. To Gabriel and to *all* his angels, he began to whisper commands:

"Angels and instruments
  Tune your music
  Soon to sing it:
Mary is bearing now
The most beautiful news for song!"

There were, in that same country, children asleep in their beds, the children who could not wake until the light came like morning into the world.

God the father was laughing now. He turned to his angels—as many angels as there are stars in the sky—and he said, "Angels?"

And the angels said, "Here, Lord. Here we are. What do you want us to do?"

"Angels go down. Down, down into the darkness to wake the children . . ."

And then it was that, like the conductor of all the world when all the world plays a mighty music, God raised his arms and sang:

> "Whistle on wooden pipes:
>   Wake the children!
>   Wake the children!
> Plead on the wailing reed
> That the children arise and come.
>
> "Organ, send forth a chord
>   Through the morning
>   And their sleeping;
> Pour in their souls the gold
> Of the light of the rising sun.
>
> "Bugle! Oh, bugle the news:
>   Last night, midnight
>   Stall and stable . . .
> Bells-bells, declaim the news:
> Lo, a baby was born! A Son!

"Bass drum and snare drum, march
    Straight to stable,
    Leading children,
Sounding their footfalls, march,
That the baby can hear them come.

"Gabriel, greet them now,
    Whisper, 'Welcome,
    All ye children.'
Angels, ignite the sky
With the fires of a midnight crown.

"Orchestras! Angels! Choirs!
    Raise a roaring,
    Glory! Glory!
Children, now round your mouths
To give praise in ten thousand tongues!

"King and his crown are here,
    Born in glory,
    Cradled poorly,
Baby shall grow to bear
On his forehead the thorns of wrong.

"Jesus! One flute alone,
    Silver singing,
    Sings to children,
Flute of five stops, his song:
'I will love you till day is done.

"'Love you until that night,
    Night of dying,
    Dies in rising.
Then in the holy dawn
I will bear you, my children, home,
In my bosom, the whole way home.'"

And it came to pass, as the angels were gone from them into heaven, that the children made haste to Bethlehem, and found Mary and Joseph, and the Babe lying in a manger. And when they had seen it, they made known abroad the saying which was told them concerning the child.

All the grinning, laughing, glad, and bright-faced children sang to the whole world the bright truth of the heavenly Father who sent his Son:

"For unto you is born this day
in the city of David
a Savior,
which is Christ the Lord!"

Every child—every son and daughter of every mother and father—shined when they sang that song. They were brighter than candles, brighter than lamps. They were as bright as the angels themselves, and the city began to see. On that Christmas morning, the children were like Christmas lights strung everywhere, in the streets and in the fields, in the houses and in the trees.

And when the children giggled, when they all began to laugh, the sun rose up in heaven, and the parents rubbed their eyes, and the people began to grin just like the children. There were presents for all the adults that morning—and the presents *were* the children!

So there was laughing and joking in all that bright land, and no one asked *Why?* any more, because everyone knew the answer.

God loved them.

God made time to tick again.

And if the children loved the Christ their Lord in return, how could the parents not love along?

Children, why this jubilee?
Why your joyous strains prolong?
What the gladsome tidings be
Which inspire your heavenly song?

Come to Bethlehem and see
Him whose birth we gladly sing;
Come adore on bended knee
Christ the Lord, the newborn king.

Gloria in excelsis Deo.
Gloria in excelsis Deo.

A Christmas Invitation

The story in this book is meant to be shared. With a real joy, Tim Ladwig and Randy Courts and I have created various ways that you might share the story with others.

Parents and Grandparents: Read!

Parents and grandparents, you will enjoy the simple, traditional pleasure of reading this book aloud. Its story—fresh yet timeless—and its dramatic pictures make the book a delight to share with children. And in this case, the story is about *your* children and how much their parents want to be with them.

Family and Friends: Act!

This story is created to start new traditions. It's written in the book somewhat like a little play to be played by all ages in the family. An adult can read the narration. Children and other adults can read the dialogue, the words of Mary and Joseph and Gabriel and God.

Arrange a set for the play: Heaven can be a sofa; Mary's house and Joseph's house two chairs; put Bethlehem in the center of the room; the fields where the littlest children (as shepherds) are all fast asleep can be all around the outside of the room. When they wake, they giggle and run to Bethlehem.

Add simple costumes for the actors, if you like: pajamas, bathrobes, towels for headpieces.

Either your actors Mary and Joseph can read their carols alone—and God can read the bits of verse he speaks; or everyone can read the carols with them. All people should read together the "Carol of the Instruments" when the children wake up.

Turn lights down at the beginning; let Gabriel bring lanterns or flashlights to Mary, to Joseph, to all the little children, which they will light and carry for the last scene at Bethlehem. And then let everyone sing favorite glad Christmas carols.

Play this play every Christmas as your family grows or as you celebrate with your extended family.

Invite close friends and other families to share it with you.

Music: Listen and Sing!

With this book also comes a CD, where we actually act out the play and sing all the music! (I read the role of the narrator and God.)

Children may just listen to the CD for their own delight (and they will, I can promise from experience, especially after they've heard the story or read the roles themselves).

But soon you and the children will learn the carols (even though they're sung on the CD by professional actors). When you can sing the carols, then your story will reach a whole new dimension of meaning: it's a musical in your home.

✦ ✦ ✦

Dear Friends:

Randy and I and college students and children and wonderful professional musicians—faithful people all—have performed *Angels and All Children* here in the Chapel of the Resurrection at Valparaiso University. Children from the cast sing it still, a year later. And we bathe in the sweetness of the experience.

We invite you to do the same.

Sunday Schools, Congregations, Grade Schools, College Drama, and Music Programs:
Scripts for the narrative and scores for the music, as these are performed on the CD, are available for public presentation of this Nativity play.

In full drama, with choirs and soloists and a chancel setting and many children in attendance (perhaps in their pajamas?) this piece makes a thrilling experience, from sin to innocence, from darkness to a genuine light.

For information about and copies of the script and score, visit my Web site: www.WalterWangerinJr.org.

CD Produced by Dewey Dellay and Randy Courts, with thanks to Greg Schaffert.
Soloists: Cass Morgan (Mary), Jeff McCarthy (Joseph), John Henry Redwood (Gabriel), Walter Wangerin, Jr. (Narrator)
Chorus: J.P. Potter, Angel Desai, Michael Frederic, Kathy Theil, Kevin Merritt, Dennis M. Hall, Juliette Hall
Instrumentalists: David Wallace, viola; Matt Beck, guitar

ANGELS AND ALL CHILDREN
A Nativity Story in Words, Music, and Art

Large-quantity purchases or custom editions of this book are available at a discount from the publisher.
For more information, contact the sales department at Augsburg Fortress, Publishers, 1-800-328-4648, or write to:
Sales Director, Augsburg Fortress, Publishers, P.O. Box 1209, Minneapolis, MN 55440-1209.

ISBN 0-8066-3712-9

Cover design by Michelle L. N. Cook and Ann Rezny; book design by Michelle L. N. Cook

The paper used in this publication meets the minimum requirements of American National Standard for Information Sciences—Permanence of Paper for Printed Library Materials, ANSI Z329.48-1984. ♾ ™

Manufactured in China   AF 9-3712

06   05   04   03   02   1   2   3   4   5   6   7   8   9   10